SpooKy
SNACKS
AND
TREATS

Spooky SNACKS AND TREATS

FRIGHTFULLY FUN
HALLOWEEN RECIPES FOR KIDS

Recipes and Photographs by
ZAC WILLIAMS

GIBBS SMITH
TO ENRICH AND INSPIRE HUMANKIND

First Edition
26 25 24 23 22   5 4 3 2 1

This book is a combination of two children's cookbooks, originally published
by Gibbs Smith as *Little Monsters Cookbook* and *Little Aliens Cookbook*.

The cooking and baking activities suggested in this book may involve the use of sharp
objects and hot surfaces. Parental or other adult guidance is recommended. The author
and publisher disclaim all responsibility of injury resulting from the performance of any
activities listed in this book. Readers assume all legal responsibility for their actions.

Published by
Gibbs Smith
P.O. Box 667
Layton, Utah 84041

1.800.835.4993 orders
www.gibbs-smith.com

Designed by Ryan Thomann and Renee Bond
Printed and bound in China

Gibbs Smith books are printed on either recycled, 100% post-consumer
waste, FSC-certified papers or on paper produced from sustainable PEFC-
certified forest/controlled wood source. Learn more at www.pefc.org.

Library of Congress Cataloging-in-Publication Data:

Names: Williams, Zac, author. | Williams, Zac, photographer.
Title: Spooky snacks and treats : frightfully fun Halloween recipes for kids /
recipes and photographs by Zac Williams.
Description: First edition. | Layton, Utah : Gibbs Smith, [2022]
Identifiers: LCCN 2021058309 | ISBN 9781423661665 (hardcover) | ISBN 9781423661672 (epub)
Subjects: LCSH: Halloween cooking. | LCGFT: Cookbooks.
Classification: LCC TX739.2.H34 W55 2022 | DDC 641.5/68—dc23/eng/20211231
LC record available at https://lccn.loc.gov/2021058309

For my little monsters,
Ethan, Rya, and Piper

CONTENTS

MUNCHIES

TREATS

THE DELICIOUSLY GRUESOME GUIDE TO
HALLOWEEN PARTY FOOD

Hosting a Halloween party is a lot of fun, but deciding on the drinks, snacks, munchies, and treats takes some work. Fortunately, in this book you will find all the recipes you need to prepare a ghastly feast for you and your creepy crew. Even those creatures of the night with particularly picky palates will find something tempting enough to sink their teeth into.

Just remember as you plan your party menu to make sure you add foods that are tasty and good for you too. Even Frankenstein's monster knows that eating right is a big part of staying fit and one step ahead of the pitchfork-carrying villagers! So try to eat all kinds of healthy foods and save the sweets for dessert.

Most importantly, the more fun you have cooking, the better the food will taste! So cook witch-style and mix it up by asking your family and friends to help with the preparation. And don't forget to serve the food with your best monster manners. Set the table in a spooky style and you are sure to freak out your guests. So get those fangs, claws, and feet ready to become a ghoulish gourmet of fine creature cuisine. Let's dig in . . . at least six feet under!

STAYING SAFE

Your blood is a very precious thing. Just ask Dracula. To preserve all of that great red stuff it is important to follow safety rules while in the kitchen. Here are important tips to keep you from getting hurt.

- Always ask an adult to help when using the stove, micro-wave, or oven. Never use a cooking range or microwave without supervision to help you avoid burns and fires.

- Knives can be very dangerous. Have a grown-up help you chop or cut any ingredients that require a sharp blade. Don't ever play with kitchen knives. They are tools for use in cooking only.

- Small kitchen appliances such as blenders and food proces-sors help make cooking easier, but they should always be used with an adult's assistance. Never put utensils or hands into these appliances.

- Wash your hands with soap and warm water before beginning to cook and wash your hands often while cooking to keep germs out of what you are making.

- Make sure to properly refriger-ate foods that can easily spoil such as meats, dairy products, eggs, and other foods that need refrigeration. This helps you avoid sickness from bacte-ria in the food.

- Never use the same plate that raw food has been on for serving food.

- Keep your kitchen work area clean and organized. Clean up spills quickly so you or some-one else doesn't slip. Keep towels and other items that could catch on fire away from the stove.

- Sometimes you might need a boost to reach the kitchen counter, but be very careful to only stand on a safe stepping stool so you don't fall.

- And most importantly, always ask for permission and help from a grown-up when you want to cook so they can make sure that you have fun in the kitchen!

MIX IT, COOK IT, CHOMP IT

Before you begin as a ghoul in the kitchen it helps to know a few things about how to cook. With a little practice, you soon will be at the head of your creepy class as an expert in the delicious dark arts! Here are some tips you should know.

MEASURING DRY INGREDIENTS: When you measure dry ingredients such as flour and sugar you will use measuring cups, usually 1 cup, $1/2$ cup, $1/3$ cup, and $1/4$ cup. Fill the correct measuring cup to the top, but not over, with your ingredient. Sometimes it helps to use a butter knife to level off the extra. Remember to keep track of how many cups you add by counting.

MEASURING LIQUID INGREDIENTS: You can use the same measuring cups that you use for dry ingredients when you measure liquids like milk or oil, but it is easier to use a clear glass measuring cup. That way you can see the liquid inside and read how much you've added to the cup by using the marks on the outside.

MEASURING WITH SPOONS: Sometimes you will need to measure ingredients in teaspoons and the bigger tablespoons. It is best to use cooking measuring spoons that are exactly the right size. If it is a dry ingredient, just add the ingredient and scrape off the extra with a butter knife until the ingredient is level with the top of the spoon.

ADDING INGREDIENTS: Have all of your ingredients out and ready to go before starting a recipe. Then add the ingredients, following the order the recipe tells you.

KEEPING CLEAN: The cleaner you keep the kitchen while you cook, the easier it is to clean up when you are done. Try to put dirty dishes and utensils in the sink as soon as you are done with them. An apron can help you keep yourself clean. Remember to wash your hands often with soap and warm water.

EXPERIMENT AND HAVE FUN: Cooking is about being creative. Maybe you'll have a great idea for something different in a recipe. You can even try mixing together your favorite flavors into a totally new combination. Have fun and keep cooking!

HOCUS POCUS
CHILLERS

This thirst quencher is a great way to beat the heat while dancing to "The Monster Mash."

MAKES 4 SERVINGS

1 quart lime sherbet

1/2 cup boysenberry syrup (pancake syrup works great)

1 liter lemon-lime soda, chilled

 1 Place 2 scoops of lime sherbet in each glass. Drizzle sherbet with boysenberry syrup.

2 Quickly fill each glass with lemon-lime soda for magic foam to appear.

DOUBLE-TROUBLE CAULDRON CONCOCTION

Mix up this cauldron of colorful punch because it is perfect for keeping a creepy crowd well hydrated.

MAKES 16 SERVINGS

2 liters lemon-lime soda, chilled

32 ounces grape juice, chilled

2 limes, sliced

1 quart lime sherbet

Fresh mint leaves

1 In a large punch bowl or cauldron, mix the lemon-lime soda and the grape juice. Add half of the lime slices to the punch.

2 Remove the lime sherbet from the freezer and allow to soften slightly. Cover the surface of the punch with scoops of sherbet. Garnish with more limes and mint leaves. Serve immediately.

MIDNIGHT MADNESS
PUNCH

When darkness descends and the stars align, quench your thirst after a late night of trick-or-treating with this punch.

MAKES 12 SERVINGS

1/2 fresh pineapple

2 liters grape soda, chilled

6 cups crushed ice

1 1/2 quarts rainbow sherbet

1 Cut the pineapple into slices about 1/2 inch thick. Using a small star-shaped cookie cutter, cut out pineapple stars.

2 Pour grape soda and crushed ice into a large punch bowl. Using different size scoops, add round balls of rainbow sherbet to the punch. Garnish with floating pineapple stars.

BUBBLING
WITCH'S BREW

Cast your colorful spell before drinking this bubbly brew and watch for the magical reaction to tickle your nose.

MAKES 4 DRINKS

Ice cubes

1 liter lemon-lime soda

Various food coloring

4 packages Pop
   Rocks candy

1 Put ice cubes in a beaker-style glass. Pour in lemon-lime soda until it is about an inch from the rim. Add a drop of your favorite fcod coloring, say a witch's spell, and stir gently. Repeat for remaining drinks.

2 Right before drinking your brew, dump in a package of Pop Rocks candy and watch the bubbling reaction!

IMPORTANT NOTE: Dry ice can be used to make fun fog effects, but *never* put dry ice into anything that will be eaten or drunk. Dry ice can be very dangerous. Children should not handle dry ice—adults only! Ask your adult helper if you want to have dry ice effects for your party.

WOLFSBANE ELIXIR

Many werewolves claim this elixir lets them retain their human shape. You might want to brew an extra batch just in case.

MAKES 2 DRINKS

Blue decorating sugar

Crushed ice

1/2 cup blue raspberry–flavored Italian syrup*

1 liter sparkling water

1/4 cup half-and-half

1 Prepare 2 glasses by wetting the rims and dipping them into the blue decorating sugar. Fill each glass 3/4 of the way full with crushed ice.

2 Add 1/4 cup blue raspberry syrup to each glass. Then fill each glass almost to the top with sparkling water.

3 Add a splash of half-and-half to each glass and enjoy!

* Any other colorful flavor may be substituted if you like.

COUNT DRACULA
CHOCOLATE SHAKE

Dracula loves chocolate, but he likes something else even more. I bet you can guess what that is! This delicious shake is certainly chocolatey, but what exactly are those red chunks??

MAKES 2 SHAKES

4 scoops vanilla ice cream

3/4 cup skim milk

4 tablespoons chocolate syrup plus more for serving

6 maraschino cherries, divided

Canned whipped cream

Grenadine syrup (optional)

1 Place the ice cream, milk, 4 tablespoons chocolate syrup, and 4 cherries in a blender. Blend on high speed until the cherries are chopped and the shake is smooth.

2 Pour the shake into 2 glasses. Garnish with whipped cream, a small drizzle of chocolate syrup, and grenadine if you wish.

3 Add a cherry on top of each and serve.

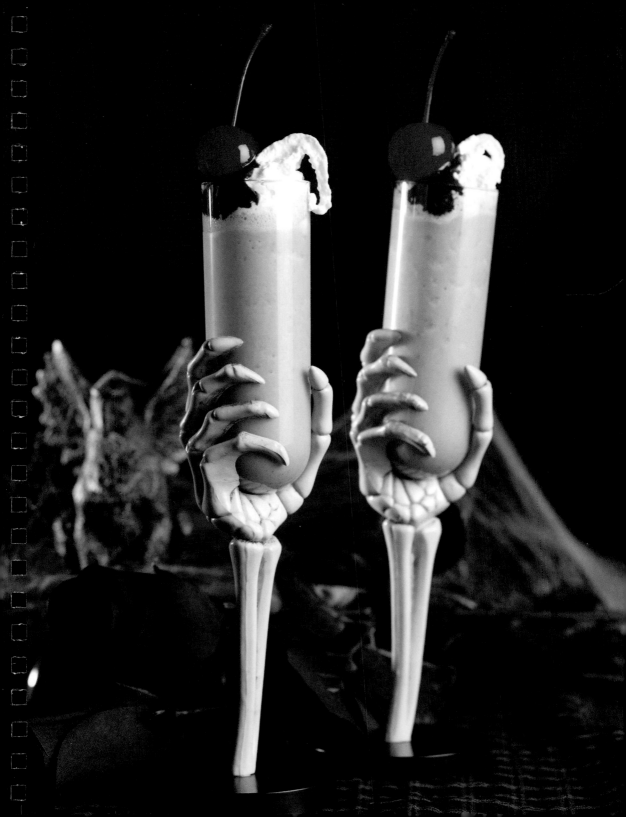

SPOOKY FONDUE

A fantastic fondue is a fun way to make fruit look spooky—just a quick dip and your strawberry is all ghostly.

MAKES 4 TO 6 SERVINGS

1 cup whipping cream

1/4 cup chocolate drink mix (such as Nesquik)

1 tablespoon peanut butter

Fruit (banana chunks, apple slices, strawberries)

Pretzels

1 Using a whisk or electric mixer, beat together the whipping cream, chocolate drink mix, and peanut butter until smooth and the cream begins to thicken.

2 Pour into a serving bowl. Dip fruit pieces using bamboo skewers or fondue forks and pretzels by hand.

MOONLIT BOG DIP

Made from ingredients straight out of a creepy bog on a full-moon night, this mossy-looking dip goes well with crunchy vegetables and crackers.

MAKES 6 SERVINGS

1 (10-ounce) package frozen chopped spinach, thawed and drained

1 1/2 cups sour cream

3/4 cup mayonnaise

1 package vegetable dip mix

Vegetables (mini carrots, cherry tomatoes, cucumber slices, broccoli florets)

Crackers

1 Place spinach, sour cream, mayonnaise, and vegetable dip mix in a medium bowl. Mix well.

2 Refrigerate for 4 hours before serving. Serve with assorted fresh vegetables, crackers, and whatever other bits of bog plants you wish.

TENTACLE TEASERS

These red-capped creepers are coming to take you away. Eat them up before they get you!

MAKES 8 SERVINGS

8 string cheese sticks

4 cherry or grape tomatoes

1 cup sun-dried tomato or herbed hummus

8 larger round whole-grain crackers

1 Pull apart the bottom ¾ of each string cheese stick to make tentacles. Cut each tomato in half.

2 Spread a spoonful of hummus on each cracker and then place a piece of cheese, with the stringy side down, on top of hummus. Top each string cheese portion with a tomato half.

VAMPIRE BITES

When the sun goes down, our friendly bloodsuckers are ready for the night shift. These little bites hit the spot when liquid nourishment is hard to find.

MAKES 8 BITES

2 medium Red Delicious apples

1/2 cup creamy peanut butter

1/2 cup slivered blanched almonds

Chocolate syrup (optional)

1 Core the apples, but don't peel them. Slice each apple into 8 wedges.

2 Spread peanut butter onto half of the apple wedges. Press slivered almonds into 1 side of each apple wedge to create scraggly teeth or to make fangs.

3 Place an apple slice with the peanut butter side up and top with another apple slice without peanut butter to form a mouth with red lips and teeth.

4 Drizzle with chocolate syrup if desired.

CORPSE FINGERS

These delicious fingers were found near some open coffins in the cemetery. They are extra tasty when dipped into red sauce.

MAKES 10 FINGERS

- 1 (4-ounce) package frozen spinach, prepared according to directions and drained
- 3/4 cup butter, softened
- 2 cups shredded sharp cheddar cheese
- 2 cups all-purpose flour
- 3/4 teaspoon salt
- 2 teaspoons Italian seasoning
- Sliced almonds
- 1 egg, beaten
- 1 cup shredded Parmesan cheese
- Marinara sauce

1 Preheat oven to 375 degrees F. Line a baking sheet with aluminum foil and spray lightly with nonstick cooking spray.

2 Chop cooked spinach into small pieces. In a large bowl, combine spinach, butter, and cheddar cheese. Beat with an electric mixer on medium speed until well blended. Add flour, salt, and Italian seasoning, a little at a time, while continuing to mix at low speed to form a soft dough.

3 Form the dough into 10 equal-size balls, then roll each ball into a log about 4 inches long. Place on the prepared baking sheet. Flatten on 1 end to form a fingertip and insert a sliced almond. Brush with egg and sprinkle with Parmesan cheese.

4 Bake for 16–18 minutes or until slightly brown. Remove from oven and serve warm with marinara sauce for dipping.

HOBGOBLIN FEET

Serve these gnarled goblin feet sandwiches to your party guests to keep them on their toes.

MAKES 6 SANDWICH FEET

Foot-shaped cookie cutter

6 slices thick, hearty bread

6 slices ham

6 slices Swiss cheese

1 tablespoon mustard

2 tablespoons mayonnaise

1 can black olives, cut in half

Leaf lettuce (optional)

1 Using a foot-shaped cookie cutter, cut out a shape from each slice of bread.

2 With the same cookie cutter, cut out a foot-shaped piece of ham and a foot-shaped piece of cheese from each slice.

3 In a small bowl, stir together the mustard and mayonnaise until well blended. Spread the mixture on each foot-shaped piece of bread. Top each with a ham and then a cheese slice. Place on a baking sheet and broil on high for 6–8 minutes or until the cheese melts.

4 Decorate with olive halves to make toes on the feet. A little dab of mustard can be used if needed to set the olives. Serve immediately on a bed of lettuce if desired.

UFOS (UNIDENTIFIED FLATBREAD OBJECTS)

These tasty flatbread objects will give you something to chew on while you consider the possibility of visitors from other worlds. Did you invite them to your Halloween party?

MAKES 8 SERVINGS

8 flatbread rounds or pitas

2 large avocados, pitted, peeled, and mashed (2 cups prepared mashed avocado may be substituted)

1 teaspoon lemon juice

1 tablespoon taco seasoning

1/4 cup sour cream

1 cup shredded cheddar cheese

1 small tomato, seeded and diced

1/2 cup black olives, cut in half

1 Preheat oven to 425 degrees F. Line 2 baking sheets with aluminum foil.

2 Using clean scissors, cut the flatbread rounds into flying saucer and alien shapes. Discard leftover bread. Place shapes on prepared baking sheets and bake for 10–12 minutes, until light brown. Remove from oven and let cool.

3 Mix mashed avocado with lemon juice, taco seasoning, and sour cream. Spread avocado mixture over each flatbread shape and top with cheese, tomatoes, and olives.

FRANKENSTEIN ZAPS

If a spark of lightning can bring Frankenstein's monster to life, just imagine what a zap can do to this delicious snack. You'll have your guests glowing like ghostly apparitions.

MAKES 4 SNACKS

2 avocados

1/4 cup sour cream

1 teaspoon lemon juice

2 tablespoons prepared mild salsa

1 bag guacamole-flavored tortilla chips*

2 cups shredded Mexican-blend cheese

1 small tomato, diced

1 Peel and pit the avocados. Chop and then mash them in a small bowl. Mix in sour cream, lemon juice, and salsa. Refrigerate for 30 minutes.

2 Arrange tortilla chips on 4 small microwave-safe plates. Sprinkle each with 1/2 cup cheese.

3 Microwave plates, 1 at a time, on high for 30 seconds or until cheese is melted and bubbly. Garnish with avocado dip and diced tomato. Serve immediately.

* Other colored tortilla chips may be substituted.

MUMMY PUPS

Mummy pups can put up quite a howl if provoked. Fortunately these little guys can be taken care of in one quick bite.

MAKES 18 TO 20 PUPS

- 1 (8-ounce) can refrigerated breadstick dough
- 1 (16-ounce) package cocktail wieners or mini hot dogs
- Mustard
- Ketchup

1 Preheat oven to 400 degrees F. Lightly spray a baking sheet with nonstick cooking spray.

2 Open the refrigerated dough and roll it out on a smooth surface. Cut each breadstick into thirds. Wrap each mini hot dog several times with a strip of dough to make mummy bandages.

3 Place mummy pups on the prepared baking sheet and bake for 8–10 minutes, until golden.

4 Let cool slightly and then add 2 drops of mustard to each for the eyes. Serve with more mustard and ketchup for dipping.

GARLICKY TOAST STAKES

What do vampires hate more than garlic? Wooden stakes, of course! Here's a tasty recipe that you'll want to serve at your party to keep the vampires away.

MAKES 18 TOAST STAKES

6 tablespoons butter or margarine, softened

1/2 teaspoon garlic powder

6 slices thick-sliced bread or Texas toast

1 cup shredded mozzarella cheese

2 tablespoons chopped parsley

1 Preheat oven to 350 degrees F. Lightly spray a baking sheet with nonstick cooking spray.

2 Place the softened butter in a small mixing bowl. Add the garlic powder and mix well. Spread the mixture evenly on 1 side of each slice of bread.

3 Trim the crusts off the bread and discard. Cut each slice of bread into thirds. Trim 1 end of each rectangle of bread into a triangle stake shape. Place the bread stakes on the prepared baking sheet.

4 Evenly sprinkle each stake with cheese and parsley.

5 Bake for 7–9 minutes, until the toast is brown and the cheese is melted. Serve warm.

COFFIN CRUNCHERS

Sometimes when you are up all night causing Halloween mischief, you just need something to tide you over till morning. This snack has a crunch that can be heard through six feet of soil.

MAKES 6 SERVINGS

6 round pita flatbreads (not pocket pita)

3 tablespoons olive oil

1 teaspoon Italian seasoning

1 cup freshly grated Parmesan cheese

2 cups hummus or marinara sauce

1 Preheat oven to 425 degrees F. Line 2 baking sheets with aluminum foil.

2 Using a knife or kitchen scissors, cut various-size coffin shapes from the pita flatbread. Discard leftover bread. Place the coffin shapes on the prepared baking sheets.

3 Lightly brush each coffin shape with olive oil. Sprinkle with Italian seasoning. Then sprinkle with Parmesan cheese and bake for 10–12 minutes, until cheese melts. Remove from oven and let cool until crunchy.

4 Serve coffin crunchers with hummus or marinara sauce for dipping.

CREEPY CLAWS
OF THE YETI

Few people know that the yeti is a Far Eastern cousin of the werewolf. Beware the yeti's claws, unless of course they happen to be these tasty party snacks.

MAKES 24 CLAWS

24 round pot sticker wrappers

1 (8-ounce) package cream cheese, softened

2 green onions, finely chopped

$\frac{1}{2}$ cup sweet-and-sour sauce, plus more for serving

4 to 6 tablespoons canola or vegetable oil

1 Open the pot sticker wrappers. In the center of a wrapper, place a spoonful of cream cheese, a few chopped green onion pieces, and a small drizzle of sweet-and-sour sauce. Moisten the edges of the wrapper with water, fold in half, and seal. Repeat for remaining pot stickers.

2 Heat the oil in a skillet over medium-high heat. Add the prepared pot stickers, 2 or 3 at a time, cooking on each side about 2 minutes, until puffy, golden, and crispy. Transfer to a plate lined with paper towels and let drain.

3 Serve immediately with more sweet-and-sour sauce for dipping.

COBWEB PARTY ROLLS

These cobweb-topped party rolls taste like donuts and are a favorite of witches and warlocks. But beware of the spider who made them.

MAKES 32 PARTY ROLLS

2 tablespoons sugar

1 teaspoon cinnamon

16 frozen roll dough pieces, thawed

1/2 cup butter, melted

1 can prepared cream cheese frosting

Assorted food coloring (neon purples, pinks, greens)

1 Line a baking sheet with parchment paper or spray with nonstick cooking spray.

2 Combine sugar and cinnamon in a small bowl. Separate each dough piece into 2 pieces. Dip each piece in melted butter and roll in sugar-and-cinnamon mixture. Place dough pieces on the prepared baking sheet and let rise for 2–3 hours or until double in size.

3 Preheat oven to 350 degrees F. Bake dough pieces for 12 minutes.

4 Place frosting in a microwave-safe container and heat on high for 30–60 seconds, stirring until smooth and runny. Separate melted frosting into 3 sandwich baggies and add a few drops of food coloring to each. Knead to mix well.

5 On a sheet of wax paper, spread out the baked rolls. With scissors, snip 1 corner off each sandwich baggie and drizzle frosting over each roll, making a cobweb pattern. Combine various frosting colors as desired. Arrange on a platter and serve.

FROG EYE NIBBLES

Brined frog eyes from the warlock's pantry make these snacks a perfect party food. They are tasty, filling, and just a little spooky because your food is watching you.

MAKES 12 SERVINGS

- 1 baguette or other loaf thin French bread
- 5 Roma tomatoes, diced
- $1/2$ teaspoon minced garlic
- 2 tablespoons olive oil
- 2 tablespoons balsamic vinegar
- 2 tablespoons chopped fresh basil
- $1/2$ teaspoon salt
- $1/2$ teaspoon black pepper
- 2 cups shredded mozzarella cheese
- 1 cup frog eyeballs (green olives with pimientos, each cut in half)

1 Preheat broiler on high. Cut baguette into 12 slices about $1/2$ inch thick. Place bread slices on a baking sheet lined with aluminum foil. Broil bread slices for about 2 minutes, until slightly brown. Remove from oven.

2 Mix tomatoes, garlic, olive oil, vinegar, basil, salt, and pepper in a bowl until combined.

3 Top each bread slice with a spoonful of tomato mixture and a sprinkle of cheese. Return to broiler for about 3 minutes or until cheese is melted and slightly browning.

4 Remove from oven and top each slice with 2 olive halves for eyeballs before serving.

SCREAMS-AFTER-DARK
SNACK MIX

What do you get when you take a little bite of this and a little bite of that? Screams after dark, of course. This sweet-and-salty snack mix is perfect to eat while watching your favorite Halloween movie with your creepy crew.

MAKES 8 SERVINGS

3 cups Rice Chex cereal

3 cups Corn Chex cereal

3/4 cup roasted salted almonds

1/4 cup butter or margarine

1/4 cup packed brown sugar

2 tablespoons honey

1 cup mini pretzel twists

1/2 cup yogurt-covered raisins

1 cup red licorice bites

1 Preheat oven to 400 degrees F. Line a baking sheet with aluminum foil and lightly spray with nonstick cooking spray. Set aside.

2 Combine the cereal and almonds in a large bowl. Set aside.

3 Place butter, brown sugar, and honey in a microwave-safe bowl. Microwave on high, covered loosely, for about 2 minutes, stirring halfway through. Carefully pour the mixture over the cereal and nuts. Stir to coat.

4 Spread the cereal mixture on the prepared baking sheet and bake for 8 minutes. Remove and let cool.

5 Put the pretzel twists, yogurt-covered raisins, and licorice bites in a large serving container. Stir in the cooled cereal.

GHOUL DROOL
SPUD SKINS

Who knew ghostly ghoul drool could taste so delicious? These topped potato skins fill tummies and help keep creatures of the night at bay.

MAKES 6 SPUD SKINS

3 large baked potatoes

3 tablespoons butter or margarine, melted and divided

3/4 teaspoon seasoned salt

3 strips bacon, cooked and crumbled

3/4 cup ghoul drool (sour cream), divided

1/2 cup grated cheddar cheese

2 tablespoons chopped chives

1 Preheat oven to 475 degrees F. Lightly spray a baking sheet with nonstick cooking spray.

2 Cut the baked potatoes in half lengthwise. Scoop out the potato insides to within about 1/2 inch of the skins. In a bowl, mix the scooped-out potato, 2 tablespoons of the melted butter, seasoned salt, crumbled bacon, and 1/2 cup of the ghoul drool (sour cream).

3 Brush the outside of the potato skins with the remaining tablespoon of butter. Spoon the potato and sour cream mixture equally into the skins. Top each with some of the grated cheddar cheese.

4 Bake the skins for 8–10 minutes or until the cheese is melted. Serve immediately, topped with the remaining ghoul drool and chives.

SAUCES
OF THE UNDEAD WITH
NUGGETS

Zombies like their food really saucy. What is better than one sauce? How about three kinds, all sure to please even the pickiest denizens of darkness?

MAKES 6 TO 8 SERVINGS

2 pounds frozen popcorn chicken or nuggets

1 cup mayonnaise, divided

2 tablespoons mustard

2 tablespoons honey

2 tablespoons chopped toasted pecans (optional)

1 (4- to 8-ounce) can crushed pineapple

3/4 cup barbecue sauce

3/4 cup buttermilk

1 tablespoon dried parsley

1/2 teaspoon black pepper

1/2 teaspoon onion powder

1 Follow the instructions on the package and bake the popcorn chicken or nuggets.

2 While the chicken is baking, prepare the three Sauces of the Undead.

3 Serve sauces and a large plate of chicken and get out of the way of those hungry zombies!

MONSTER STING SAUCE

Mix together 1/2 cup mayonnaise, 2 tablespoons mustard, and 2 tablespoons honey and blend well. Place in a small serving bowl and sprinkle with chopped toasted pecans if desired.

HOWL-AT-THE-MOON SAUCE

Open and drain the can of crushed pineapple. Mix pineapple with barbecue sauce. Place in a small serving bowl.

PALE-FACED BUTTERMILK SAUCE

Combine 1/2 cup mayonnaise, buttermilk, parsley, pepper, and onion powder. Mix well and refrigerate for at least 30 minutes. Place in a small serving bowl.

FULL-MOON HOWLERS

When you're out running with the pack under a full moon, these delicious two-bite sandwiches are just what the partiers crave to quiet a growling stomach.

MAKES 12 MINI SANDWICHES

24 precooked frozen meatballs

1 cup ketchup

1/4 cup packed brown sugar

1 teaspoon mustard

12 small buns or dinner rolls

Lettuce

Tiny dill pickles

1 Heat the frozen meatballs in the microwave or oven, following the package directions. Make sure the meatballs are completely heated throughout.

2 Add ketchup, brown sugar, and mustard to a large saucepan over medium heat. Cook and stir until the sauce just begins to boil. Remove from heat. Add the heated meatballs and stir to coat the meatballs with the sauce.

3 Place 2 meatballs on each bun or roll. Add a leaf of lettuce and a pickle on top. Serve immediately.

EYE-OF-NEWT
SALAD

This tasty salad is great for when you need to use up leftovers from the witch's cottage storeroom. Don't you just love a plate of nice, juicy eyeballs?

MAKES 6 TO 8 SERVINGS

1 pound green seedless grapes

1 pound red seedless grapes

1 cup sour cream

1 (8-ounce) package cream cheese, softened

1/2 cup packed brown sugar

1/2 teaspoon vanilla extract

1 to 2 drops green food coloring

Grenadine syrup

Bamboo skewers

1 Wash and remove the grapes from the stems and set aside.

2 In a large serving bowl, mix the sour cream, cream cheese, brown sugar, and vanilla together. Stir in food coloring.

3 Fold the grapes into this mixture. Refrigerate, covered, for at least 2 hours before serving.

4 Spoon into bowls and drizzle with grenadine syrup. Serve with bamboo skewers for stabbing the eyeballs.

WORMS AND THINGS SALAD

This deliciously refreshing graveyard salad is so fun to slurp. A few slippery, slimy creatures might be lurking in there as well.

MAKES 8 TO 10 SERVINGS

1 (16-ounce) package spaghetti

1 cup wagon-wheel pasta

1 Roma tomato, chopped

1 cup cubed cheddar cheese

1 cucumber, peeled and chopped

1 cup green olives with pimientos

1 (16-ounce) bottle low-fat Italian dressing

Salad seasoning

1 Following the package directions, boil the spaghetti, drain, and rinse with cold water. In a separate pan, boil the wagon wheel pasta, drain, and rinse with cold water. Place both pastas in a chilled serving bowl.

2 Add the tomato, cheese, cucumber, and olives. Pour in the Italian salad dressing and season to taste with salad seasoning.

3 Place the salad in the refrigerator overnight to marinate. Serve cold or at room temperature.

MISTY GRAVEYARD
CHOWDER

Perfect for when you and your ghoulish grubbies
are chilled to the bone after late-night scavenging
at the graveyard for "spare" parts.

MAKES 4 SERVINGS

1 tablespoon butter

1/2 cup chopped onion

1 1/2 cups water

2 cups chopped red
potatoes, with skins

1 cup sliced carrots

1/4 teaspoon black pepper

1/2 teaspoon salt

1 (15-ounce) can corn

1/2 cup diced ham
(optional)

1 tablespoon flour

1 cup heavy cream, chilled

1 cup grated cheddar
cheese

1/2 cup sour cream

1 In a medium saucepan over medium heat, add the butter and onion. Cook, stirring frequently, until the onion is soft but not brown. Add water, potatoes, carrots, pepper, and salt.

2 Cover and simmer for about 15 minutes or until potatoes and carrots are tender.

3 Drain the can of corn. Add corn and ham, if using, to the chowder.

4 In a separate bowl, mix the flour into the cream and then slowly pour the mixture into the chowder while stirring. Continue to simmer, stirring frequently. When the chowder is thickened and bubbly, it is ready to serve.

5 Ladle chowder into bowls and garnish with grated cheese and a dollop of sour cream.

SWAMP GOBLIN GUMBO

Down in the bayou, in the deepest, swampiest, most—monster infested part, this hearty gumbo warms up the most cowardly of hearts.

MAKES 8 SERVINGS

1 pound ground turkey

1 small onion, chopped

1/2 teaspoon black pepper

1/2 teaspoon salt

1 teaspoon garlic powder

1/4 cup butter or margarine

1/3 cup flour

3 cups hot water

2 beef bouillon
   cubes, crushed

1 green bell pepper,
   seeded and chopped

3 stalks celery, chopped

1 tablespoon dried parsley

2 tablespoons
   Worcestershire sauce

1 (14.5-ounce) can diced
   tomatoes, with liquid

4 cups cooked white rice

1 In a skillet over medium-high heat, cook the ground turkey, breaking it apart. Add the chopped onion, pepper, salt, and garlic powder; cook for about 10 minutes or until the turkey is no longer pink. Drain the fat and set the mixture aside.

2 In a large, heavy stockpot, melt the butter over medium-high heat. Sprinkle with the flour and whisk to form a paste. Slowly stir in the hot water and crushed bouillon cubes.

3 Add the chopped green pepper and celery along with the parsley and Worcestershire sauce. Bring the mixture to a boil.

4 Add the cooked ground turkey and canned tomatoes. Cover and simmer for 15 minutes.

5 Place a ladle of gumbo in a bowl over 1/2 cup cooked white rice for each person.

WRAP LIKE A MUMMY

This recipe is great for special occasions like Halloween or maybe even Mummy's Day. Be sure to eat it while it's hot—unlike the real thing, you won't want to leave it sitting around for thousands of years!

MAKES 4 SERVINGS

1 package frozen puff pastry sheets

1 cup chopped cooked chicken breast

1 cup sliced button mushrooms

1/2 cup frozen green peas

1/4 cup Alfredo sauce

1 cup freshly grated Parmesan cheese

1 orange or yellow bell pepper

1 Preheat oven to 375 degrees F. Spray a baking sheet with nonstick cooking spray. Place 1 sheet of puff pastry dough on the counter for 45 minutes, until thawed.

2 Unfold the pastry sheet to form a flattened rectangle of dough. Using a knife or kitchen shears, start on the left edge of dough and cut 1/2-inch-wide strips one third of the way in toward the center. Repeat on the right edge of the dough, cutting 1/2-inch-wide strips one third of the way toward the center.

3 On the uncut center of the pastry, spread the chicken, mushrooms, and peas. Pour the Alfredo sauce evenly across the ingredients. Set aside 2 tablespoons of Parmesan cheese and sprinkle the remaining cheese over the chicken mixture.

4 Beginning at the bottom, fold over the strips of pastry to the center, alternating sides. This will create a bandaged look. Shape the filled dough with your hands to look like a mummy's body.

5 Place on prepared baking sheet. Sprinkle the remaining Parmesan cheese over the mummy. Bake for 16–18 minutes or until brown and puffy.

6 Decorate with bell pepper slices and pieces cut out in shapes for the eyes and mouth. Serve immediately.

WIZARD'S PIZZA

When a wizard invites his broom-flying friends over for a pizza bake, he lets everyone choose their own toppings from his carefully curated cupboard. You can do the same for your party.

MAKES 8 INDIVIDUAL PIZZAS

Beast bites (pepperoni)

Smoked werewolf (ham or Canadian bacon slices)

Toadstool morsels (sliced button mushrooms)

Tarantula eggs (black olives)

Paleapple (pineapple chunks)

Igor's delight (sliced green bell peppers)

Frog eyeballs (green olives)

Blood berries (sliced cherry tomatoes)

8 round pitas (not pocket pita)

1 (12-ounce) jar pizza sauce

2 cups shredded mozzarella cheese

Essence of immortality (Italian seasoning)

1 Place each pizza topping in its own bowl or jar on a table or counter. A label identifying each dreadful ingredient is always fun.

2 Spread aluminum foil on the bottom oven rack. Preheat oven to 450 degrees F.

3 Place each pita on a plate and spread with 2 tablespoons of pizza sauce. Sprinkle with 1/4 cup cheese.

4 Allow guests to decorate their pizzas with whichever ingredients they choose. Sprinkle with Italian seasoning.

5 Place pizzas in the oven directly on the top oven rack. Bake for 5–6 minutes, until bubbly and crisp.

BLOODCURDLING BRAIN LOAVES

This hearty party munchie comes straight from the laboratory, using leftover bits of this and that to form the perfect brain food.

MAKES 6 SERVINGS

- 1 1/2 pounds lean ground beef
- 1 cup finely crushed saltine crackers
- 3/4 cup ketchup
- 1 small onion, finely chopped
- 2 tablespoons Worcestershire sauce
- 1 teaspoon salt
- 1/2 teaspoon black pepper
- 1 egg, beaten
- 1 (18-ounce) bottle barbecue sauce, or more to taste
- Green olives

1 Preheat oven to 350 degrees F. Cover a baking sheet with aluminum foil lightly sprayed with nonstick cooking spray.

2 In a mixing bowl, combine ground beef, crackers, ketchup, onion, Worcestershire sauce, salt, pepper, and egg. Mix well until combined.

3 Place half the mixture in a heavy zip-top freezer baggie. Cut off a corner of the baggie and squeeze out mixture into 3 brain shapes. Repeat with remaining mixture. Pour enough barbecue sauce on the meat loaves to cover them completely. Add green olives for eyes.

4 Bake for 40 minutes or until an instant-read thermometer inserted in the middle of meat loaves registers 160 degrees F. Serve with more barbecue sauce if desired.

HAUNTED HOUSE
LASAGNA

Moldy green lasagna can't be beat for serving in a haunted house. Beware of who might be lurking behind you, wanting to take a bite.

MAKES 8 SERVINGS

1 (16-ounce) package
   lasagna noodles

1 tablespoon olive oil

1 small onion, chopped

1 (12-ounce) package
   frozen spinach, thawed

1 (10-ounce) bottle
   prepared pesto

1 (24-ounce) container
   cottage cheese

1 egg

1 teaspoon salt

3/4 teaspoon black pepper

2 tablespoons Italian
   seasoning

3 cups shredded
   mozzarella cheese

1 (8-ounce) jar prepared
   Alfredo sauce

1 Prepare lasagna noodles according to package directions. Drain and rinse. Preheat oven to 350 degrees F. Spray a 9 x 13-inch baking dish with nonstick cooking spray.

2 In a large skillet, heat olive oil over medium heat, adding onion and stirring until translucent. Add spinach and pesto and continue heating until hot.

3 In a bowl, mix cottage cheese, egg, salt, pepper, and Italian seasoning. In prepared baking dish, layer noodles, spinach mixture, cottage cheese mixture, and mozzarella. Repeat with another layer and finish with noodles on top. Spread Alfredo sauce on top of noodles.

4 Cover with aluminum foil and bake for 40 minutes. Remove foil and continue to bake 10–15 additional minutes, until cheese is melted and bubbly.

GREEN SLIME

A secret shipment to Area 51 was misdirected to your kitchen just in time for your party. It probably isn't radioactive.

MAKES 16 SERVINGS

4 envelopes unflavored gelatin

2 cups cold water

1 cup sweetened condensed milk

2½ cups boiling water

2 (6-ounce) packages lime-flavored gelatin

16 alien or creature gummy candies

1 Lightly spray a 9 x 13-inch pan with nonstick cooking spray.

2 In a saucepan, combine unflavored gelatin with cold water. Heat over low heat, stirring until dissolved. Remove from heat and stir in condensed milk. Pour into the prepared pan and refrigerate for 45 minutes or until set.

3 While waiting, add boiling water to the lime-flavored gelatin in a large bowl. Stir until completely dissolved. After the mixture cools, pour over the set gelatin in the pan.

4 Refrigerate gelatin for 5 minutes or until slightly set. Place gummy candies in the gelatin so when you cut it to serve there will be a candy in the center of every square. Refrigerate 30 more minutes or until firm. Cut into squares and serve.

ZUPPA DI ZOMBIE

Surprise your zombie friends with this sweet dessert. It tastes much better than brains.

MAKES 6 SERVINGS

1 (3.4-ounce) package instant pistachio pudding

1 cup whipping cream

3 tablespoons powdered sugar

1/2 teaspoon vanilla extract

Blue food coloring

6 sponge cake rounds

Monster-themed breakfast cereal (such as Boo Berry or Count Chocula)*

Decorating sprinkles

1 Following the package directions, prepare the pistachio pudding and refrigerate. In a chilled bowl, combine the whipping cream, powdered sugar, and vanilla. Beat with a wire whisk or electric mixer until peaks begin to form. Add a drop or two of blue food coloring.

2 Place 1 cake round in a small glass dish. Spoon about 1/3 cup of pudding onto the cake. Sprinkle the edges with monster cereal. Top with a dollop of whipped cream and sprinkles. Repeat for remaining cakes.

* Other sweet breakfast cereal may be substituted.

EXTRATERRESTRIAL CUPCAKES

When you are planning an out-of-this-world party, take it to another level with these extra-delicious cupcakes.

MAKES 18 CUPCAKES

1 (15.25-ounce) box cake mix of choice

1 (16-ounce) can frosting of choice

Powdered sugar

1 (17.6-ounce) package Wilton Decorator Preferred Rolled Fondant in primary colors, or premade fondant of choice

Candy eyes (optional)

1 Prepare cake mix according to directions for making cupcakes. Bake and let cool completely. Frost with desired frosting.

2 On a surface dusted with powdered sugar, roll out the fondant to about 1/4 inch thick. Using a circular cookie cutter slightly larger than the size of a cupcake, cut out circles of fondant. Slide circles off the surface and cover each cupcake, slightly pulling down on edges to smooth. The frosting will help the fondant stick.

3 Using other colors of fondant rolled out to 1/4 inch thick, use mini cookie cutters or a knife to cut out shapes for eyes, noses, mouths, and hair. Press face shapes onto fondant-covered cupcakes. Candy eyes can also be gently pressed into fondant. Fondant dries quickly, so keep it covered unless directly working with it.

CREATURE CUPCAKES

For a monstrously good time, channel your inner mad scientist to bake up these little Frankenstein's monster treats for your party.

MAKES 18 CUPCAKES

- 1 (15.25-ounce) box chocolate cake mix
- 1 (16-ounce) package white candy coating or almond bark
- Green food coloring
- 1 bag large marshmallows
- 1/2 teaspoon almond extract
- 1 (16-ounce) can chocolate frosting
- Assorted decorating frostings and gels
- Green Mike and Ike candies
- Assorted candies and sprinkles

1 Prepare cake mix according to directions for making cupcakes. Line cupcake pans with fun cupcake papers and fill each two-thirds of the way full. Bake according to instructions. Let cupcakes cool.

2 Following the package directions, melt the candy coating in the microwave. After the coating is melted, add a few drops of green food coloring and stir. Add more if needed, until the candy coating is a nice monster green.

3 Using a bamboo skewer, dip a marshmallow into the candy coating until covered. Place on wax paper to let cool. Repeat until you have made 18 coated marshmallows.

4 Stir almond extract into the chocolate frosting. Then frost each cupcake.

5 Place 1 coated marshmallow in the center of each cupcake. Decorate with frosting and gels to create a mini Frankenstein's monster head. Use a little extra frosting to stick green Mike and Ike candy "bolts" to the sides of the head. Finish off with more candies and sprinkles.

WEREWOLF CUPCAKES

The secret to becoming a werewolf is to be bitten by a werewolf. While most people find that they are quite happy to remain human, these cupcakes are perfect for those who thirst for a life on the wild and hairy side.

MAKES 18 TO 24 CUPCAKES

1 (15.25-ounce) box devil's food cake mix

2 to 3 cups shredded coconut

1 (8-ounce) jar seedless raspberry jam

1 (16-ounce) can cream cheese frosting

Assorted decorating frostings and gels

1 Prepare cake mix according to directions for making cupcakes. Bake and let cool.

2 Preheat oven to 400 degrees F. Place coconut in a shallow baking dish and toast for about 5–7 minutes. You will need to have your adult supervisor help you stir the coconut a few times during the baking process until it is brown.

3 Microwave the raspberry jam in a glass bowl on high for 30 seconds. Stir until smooth. Set aside 2 tablespoons of jam in a separate bowl.

4 Using a small paring knife, cut a circular wedge out of the top of each cupcake. Spoon some raspberry jam in each and replace the top parts of the cupcakes.

5 Frost the cupcakes with the cream cheese frosting. Top with toasted coconut. Use decorator frostings and gels to create ears, eyes, nose, mouth, and fangs. Add reserved raspberry jam on the tips of the werewolves' fangs.

ONE-EYED CRAWLER CAKES

Here's looking at you! These creepy crawlers might just skitter right off of the table if you aren't careful.

MAKES 24 CUPCAKES

1 (15.25-ounce) box Funfetti cake mix

1 (16-ounce) can vanilla frosting

Neon food coloring (blue, green, purple)

24 mini white powdered donuts

Red decorating gel

24 gumdrops or gummy Lifesaver candies

24 brown mini M&M's

Multicolored licorice twists

1 Prepare cake mix according to directions for making cupcakes. Bake and let cool.

2 Divide the frosting into 3 small bowls. Add a few drops of food coloring to each and mix well. Frost the cupcakes using the different frostings.

3 On each mini donut, draw lines with the decorating gel to look like a bloodshot eye.

4 In the center of each donut place a gumdrop or gummy candy, securing it with a little bit of decorating gel. Add a brown mini M&M for the pupil.

5 Place 1 donut eye in the center of each cupcake. Use the licorice to create creepy-crawly legs. Devour them before they devour you!

BLOODY SUNDAE

The secret ingredient of this sundae is not what you might think! But it certainly will please your vampire pals.

MAKES 6 SUNDAES

6 chocolate-covered grasshopper cookies

$1/2$ cup vanilla frosting

Red food coloring

Strawberry syrup

1 quart vanilla ice cream

Canned whipped cream

Sprinkles

1 Using a pointed cookie cutter such as a star shape, cut 2 fang marks out of each cookie. Set aside cookies to use as a garnish. Save the cutout parts and any extra crumbled cookie.

2 Microwave the vanilla frosting on high for 30 seconds. Stir in several drops of red food coloring. Drizzle the chocolate cookies with the frosting. Place on wax paper in the fridge to set.

3 Drizzle strawberry syrup on the insides and bottom of a clear ice cream dish or soda glass. Add 2 scoops of vanilla ice cream. Drizzle with more strawberry syrup and top with the cookie crumbles. Garnish with a shot of whipped cream, sprinkles, and a "bitten" chocolate cookie. Repeat for remaining 5 sundaes. Serve immediately.

TRIFLE WITH DEATH

Here's a new twist on a traditional favorite. Best enjoyed in a dank crypt while plundering treasure.

MAKES 8 TO 10 SERVINGS

1 (11-ounce) prepared angel food or sponge cake

1 (6-ounce) box lime-flavored gelatin

1 cup mini marshmallows

1 small box instant vanilla pudding

Gummy worms, spiders, frogs, and other gummy candies

2 cups crushed chocolate sandwich cookies

1 Tear the cake into pieces about 1 inch in size. Place the cake pieces in the bottom of a glass trifle bowl or other large clear serving bowl.

2 Following the package directions, prepare the gelatin. Pour into the trifle bowl over the cake pieces. Sprinkle the marshmallows over the top.

3 Following the package directions, prepare the pudding. Pour the pudding over the gelatin and cake in the serving bowl. Refrigerate for at least 2 hours or until the gelatin is set.

4 Using the gummy creatures and the cookie crumbs, decorate the top of the trifle. Spread the cookie crumbs for dirt and make it look really spooky with worms and creepy candy coming out of the ground!

PURPLE PEOPLE EATER

No one is really sure what the purple people eater looks like since if you see him it is usually way too late. Now you can be the people eating the purple eater!

MAKES 6 SERVINGS

1 can boysenberry
   pie filling

2 cups biscuit mix
   (Bisquick works great)

1 cup milk

1/2 cup butter, melted

Purple decorator's sugar

1/2 pint whipping cream

2 tablespoons sugar

1/2 teaspoon vanilla

Purple sprinkles

1 Preheat oven to 375 degrees F. Spray an 8 x 8-inch baking dish with nonstick cooking spray.

2 Pour the boysenberry pie filling into the prepared baking dish. In a medium bowl, mix together the biscuit mix, milk, and butter, forming a soft dough. Spoon dough onto pie filling. Sprinkle with decorator's sugar.

3 Bake for 25–30 minutes, until fruit bubbles and topping is golden brown.

4 While the dessert is baking, whisk whipping cream, sugar, and vanilla in a chilled bowl until soft peaks form.

5 Scoop individual servings into bowls, top with whipped cream, and scatter with purple sprinkles.

DUSTY OLD BONES

Your werewolf guests might really appreciate having some bones to gnaw on while waiting for the moon to rise. These old bones are so delicious the other guests will like them as well.

MAKES 24 COOKIES

COOKIES

2 cups sugar

2 eggs

1 cup shortening, melted

1 cup evaporated milk

2 teaspoons baking
    powder

1 teaspoon salt

1 teaspoon lemon extract

5 1/2 cups flour

Powdered sugar

Bone-shaped cookie cutter

FROSTING

1/4 cup butter or
    margarine, softened

1/4 teaspoon salt

1/2 teaspoon vanilla extract

3 to 4 cups powdered
    sugar

Milk

1/4 cup cocoa powder

1/4 cup powdered sugar

Decorating gel or frosting
    (black, purple, or brown)

1 In a large bowl, mix together the sugar, eggs, and shortening until smooth and blended. Add the evaporated milk, baking powder, salt, and lemon extract, stirring well. Mix in the flour, 1 cup at a time, until the dough is stiff and can be shaped. Cover dough and refrigerate for at least 1 hour or up to 1 day.

2 Preheat oven to 400 degrees F. Roll out the dough on a smooth surface dusted with powdered sugar until it is about 1/2 inch thick. Using a bone-shaped cookie cutter, cut out cookies and place them on an ungreased baking sheet.

3 Bake cookies for 7–9 minutes, until puffy and ever so slightly brown on the edges. Remove from oven and let cool on a wire rack.

4 To make the frosting, combine the butter, salt, and vanilla in a medium bowl. Add powdered sugar, 1 cup at a time, beating until frosting is the desired consistency. Add a few drops of milk if the frosting is too thick.

5 In a small bowl, combine cocoa powder with 1/4 cup powdered sugar. Frost each bone with frosting and dust with the cocoa mixture for an old decayed look. Outline and draw cracks on the bones with the decorating gel. Serve in a big heap.

ABOUT THE AUTHOR

ZAC WILLIAMS is a partner at Williams Visual, a creative communications company. He has been the principal photographer of more than 200 books, and explores food and culture through writing and photography. He is the author of five cookbooks, including *Hungry Campers*, *French Fries*, and *Little Cowpokes Cookbook*. Zac and his family live in Eden, Utah.

METRIC CONVERSION CHART

VOLUME MEASUREMENTS		WEIGHT MEASUREMENTS		TEMPERATURE CONVERSION	
U.S.	METRIC	U.S.	METRIC	FAHRENHEIT	CELSIUS
1 teaspoon	5 ml	½ ounce	15 g	250	120
1 tablespoon	15 ml	1 ounce	30 g	300	150
¼ cup	60 ml	3 ounces	90 g	325	160
⅓ cup	75 ml	4 ounces	115 g	350	180
½ cup	125 ml	8 ounces	225 g	375	190
⅔ cup	150 ml	12 ounces	350 g	400	200
¾ cup	175 ml	1 pound	450 g	425	220
1 cup	250 ml	2 ¼ pounds	1 kg	450	230